SKYBOUND!

STARRING

MARY MYERS

AS

CARLOTTA

DAREDAVIL AERONAUT and SCIENTIST

WRITTEN BY

Sue Ganz-Schmitt

ILLUSTRATED BY

Jacopo Bruno

CALKINS CREEK
AN IMPRINT OF ASTRA BOOKS FOR YOUNG READERS
New York

*There are times
when one has to decide what to do
and do it in the twinkling of an eye.*

Mary Myers as Carlotta

Mary Breed Hawley had lofty ideas! But when she soared into the world in 1850, girls were taught not to do brave and dangerous things.

Proper young ladies like Mary were simply expected to land a husband, have children, and stay tethered to their homes.

Proper or not, Mary dreamed
of flying . . .

floating

freely

in space.

When she woke up, Mary was
still—earthbound.

Lana's Aeronautic Machine

Blanchard's Balloon

Journal des Voyages

Charles & Roberts' Balloon

Garnerin Ascending

Mary soon found ways to get her feet off the ground.
Balloon madness sailed in from France and captivated
America. Daredevil aeronauts landed on the front pages.
Ballooning! Could it be Mary's way up?

By twenty-one, Mary caught the eye of a photographer, inventor, engineer, and scientist. Carl Myers was mad about ballooning and weather. He found Mary lively and whip smart, and he swept her away with his **high-in-the-sky** ideas.

Just as society expected, Mary and Carl tied the knot.

Marriage Certificate

THIS CERTIFIES,

That Carl Edgar Myers of Abram Myers and Ann Eliza Myers and Mary Breed Hawley of John Berry Hawley and Elizabeth A. Hawley were United in the **BONDS OF MARRIAGE** on Hornellville the 8th day of November 1871 comformably to the Ordinance of God, and the Law of the State of New York

Witness: _____   Witness: _____

The new Mrs. Myers did not settle into the kitchen or the garden. Instead, she **flung** herself into Carl's library.

Mary read about aeronautics and meteorology until her head **spun** with facts. Then she helped Carl invent a **groundbreaking** balloon fabric.

Making balloon fabric may not sound dangerous, but it was chancy. The creative concoction of boiled linseed oil and turpentine could explode at any moment.

And, **oh blazes!** Sometimes it did! This didn't stop Mary. She stirred the pot until it was just right!

PROF. WAILIKY RULSON

When their first balloon was ready and the gas held fast, Mary and Carl hired a brave aeronaut to test it.
Good golly, it flew!

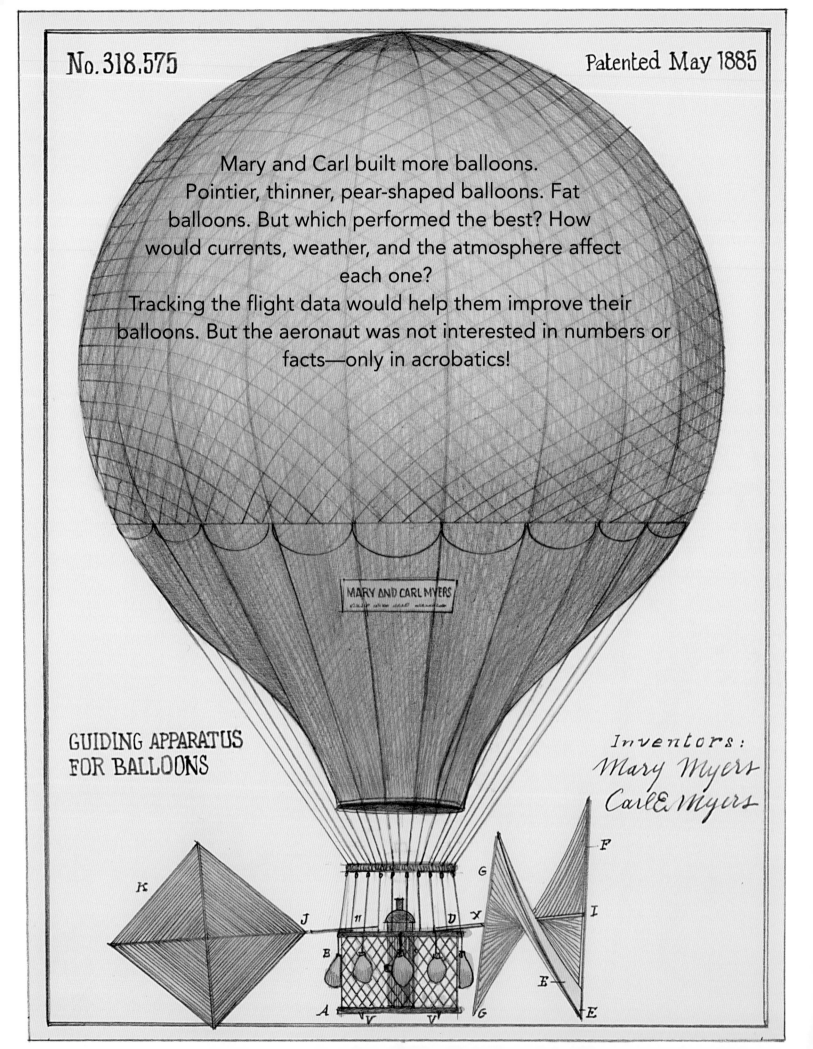

No. 318,575

Patented May 1885

Mary and Carl built more balloons. Pointier, thinner, pear-shaped balloons. Fat balloons. But which performed the best? How would currents, weather, and the atmosphere affect each one?
Tracking the flight data would help them improve their balloons. But the aeronaut was not interested in numbers or facts—only in acrobatics!

MARY AND CARL MYERS

GUIDING APPARATUS FOR BALLOONS

Inventors:
Mary Myers
Carl E. Myers

Mary and Carl realized they needed two flight professionals in one. Someone who could record the scientific data *and* **electrify** the paying crowds at fairs. (Building better balloons cost money, after all!)

Mary **lit up!** She could do both!

At first Carl didn't take his wife seriously. So Mary made a list of reasons why she was the best person for the job. And Carl was sold!

If Mary was to capture the science and captivate a crowd, she'd need a stunning new outfit and a stage name. Something exotic, yet familiar.

From now on, everyone would call her . . .

At first, she was buoyant! But as the weekend crept closer, Carlotta's mood plummeted. She'd promised to pilot her balloon one mile up. *And* to stay aloft for five miles or thirty minutes. With zero flight experience, a lot could go wrong.

Carlotta dissolved her dark clouds by imagining herself dancing with the currents over an enchanted view of Earth. Then . . .

"The day came," she noted, "a misty, moisty, miserable, rainy 'Fourth,' dampening all my expectations of a delightful tour."

The aeronaut arrived and gave Carlotta a ten-minute training on how to solo pilot a balloon.

Ten minutes to know how to steer clear of telegraph lines, steeples, and towering trees. How to track the ground below for a safe landing spot, not marshy or too near thick forests. When to release gas to go down or sprinkle sand to go higher. Ten minutes to know—how NOT to smash her balloon to bits.

Gloomy skies didn't stop folks from arriving. They spilled out of the fairgrounds and onto the streets. They squeezed together on rooftops.

They came to see the mystery person—

a woman!—daring to solo pilot a gas balloon.

In all their born days, few (if any) had seen such a thing.

Carlotta was on pins and needles.

What if her first flight was a fizzle?

The damp crowd watched Carl and his team fill the balloon. The rain stuttered against it.

Finally, the sky cleared.

Carlotta debuted with a **razzle-dazzle**. She stepped into her tiny basket. Eight of her pet homing pigeons dangled aboard.

"Let go!" she shouted.

The crew released the lines, and Carlotta set four pigeons free.

They flapped off to her hometown of Mohawk with messages announcing that Carlotta was . . .

She waved at the crowds. They waved their handkerchiefs back at her, like thousands of tiny flags saluting a new queen. Carlotta floated toward the sun. *"What a sea of faces!"* she thought.

Up.

Over "white houses, and somber roofs," then "emerald green fields and forests."

Up.

Up.

Up.

Five hundred feet.

Two thousand feet.

One mile up. "The earth is a picture painted for beauty," she admired.

Then she got busy.

Carlotta mapped the currents, kept an eagle eye on her barometer and altimeter, and collected the science of the skies.

She checked her compass and piloted her balloon on the wings of the east wind.

Soon Carlotta got swallowed by cold, damp clouds. Endless clouds with no silver linings. The "milk-white mist . . . chilled like the grasp of an icy hand."

Carlotta checked her altimeter.

Two miles up!

The remaining four frigid pigeons fell silent in their cages.

Carlotta could not see earth, sky, or balloon. It was the "lonesomest place" she had ever been.

She wanted out from the grip of the **ghost clouds**. The temperature grew icier and her balloon felt frozen in space. But Carlotta's compass told her the balloon raced on . . .

Spinning.
Spinning.
Spinning.

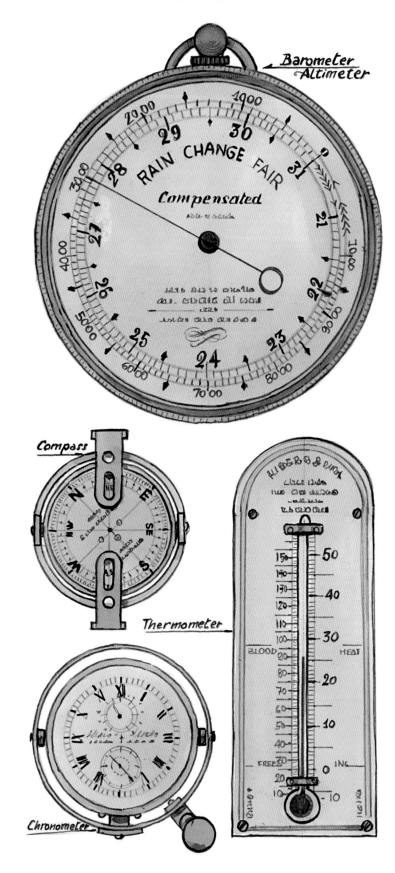

Barometer Altimeter

Compass

Chronometer

Thermometer

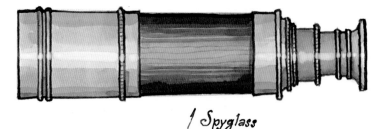

Spyglass

And suddenly . . .
The clouds parted like curtains releasing a star to the sky:

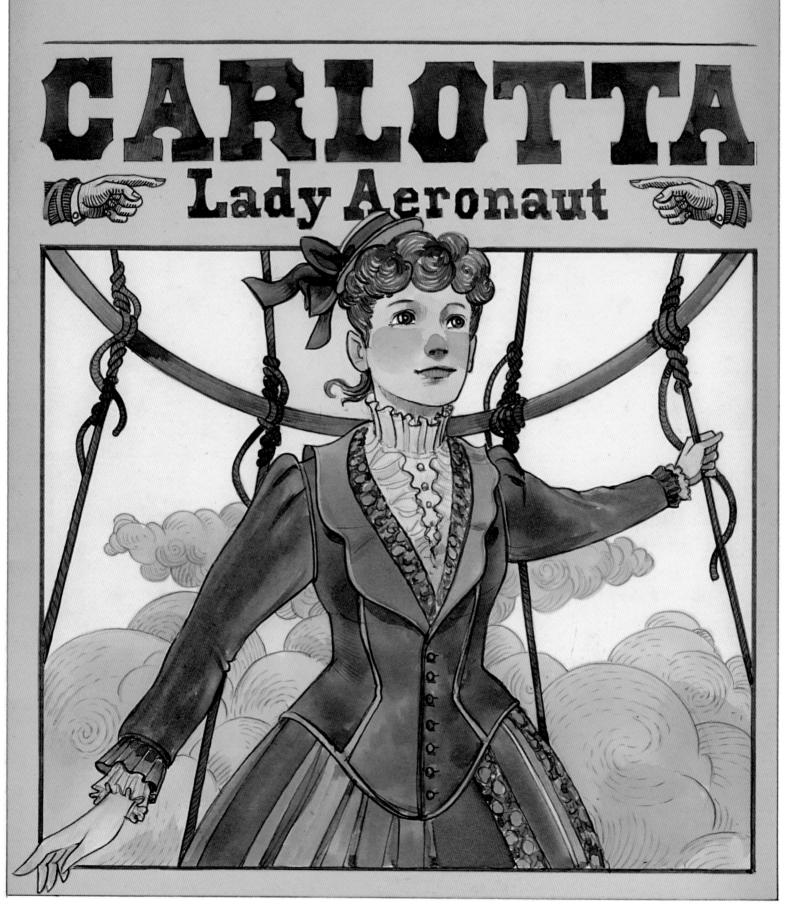

CARLOTTA
Lady Aeronaut

Carlotta glimpsed the blanket of beautiful earth below.

Land sakes! An open field!

She attached messages to two pigeons, with word of her descent.

Carlotta tugged her gas valve open.

Down.
Down.
Down.
She set the final two pigeons free with the news she'd landed.

Carlotta had sailed two miles up for twenty miles. *And* she'd stayed in the air for thirty-five minutes. Higher, longer, and farther than expected.

Huzzah! She'd brought down the data on currents, weather, and atmospheric pressure—clues to her flight success.

The slack-jawed farmer who found Carlotta told her that she was "most too young a girl to be trusted so far from home."

Not to be trusted?

A daredevil woman—who fished alone in the sky for science? And wrestled with ghost clouds?

That farmer was right—she should go back home. It was the perfectly proper thing for a lady like her to do . . .

. . . **a lady aeronaut**, who needed to plan her next flight.

Carlotta in her balloon basket at Congress Park in Saratoga Springs, New York. Carl front right.

MORE ABOUT CARLOTTA

Carlotta commuted from noisy fairgrounds filled with bands, bravado, and adoring crowds . . . up and away to her sky-quiet laboratory. Alone, or with her dog Columbia, she tested new shapes and sizes of balloons. She studied the location and flow of air currents—her findings helped her zigzag through them like a graceful dragonfly.

She also tested different fuels in the balloons including hot air, coal gas, hydrogen, water gas, and natural gas (these last two were first used by the Myerses). The Myerses' experiments showed hydrogen to be the best fuel of their time. In their gas-tight balloons, hydrogen could last for days, had great lifting power, and was easily made from water, sulphuric acid, and iron filings. Carlotta helped Carl design his patented portable gas device, which the couple took from town to town for anytime-anywhere liftoffs. This made it possible for Carlotta to launch at two fairs in different cities on the same day. The Myerses shared their mechanical and meteorological findings generously with the scientific and aeronautic community. They also shared their findings publicly, hoping to educate and excite the world.

Sometimes, though, Carlotta secretly snuck new equipment into her basket for testing up high—leading to aeronautic breakthroughs. One such craft she and Carl designed was guided by a screw propeller made with fabric. This allowed Carlotta to steer the craft, flying and landing just about anywhere she pleased. They patented the device, and Carlotta officially became one of the few women inventors of her time.

EVEN MORE ABOUT CARLOTTA!

A historical account of the Lady Aeronaut's excellent skills explains that "Carlotta had to estimate and control with split-second accuracy wind drift, rate of fall, and amount of sideways glide, and make them all come out even at just one point. She was not only daring and pretty; she was something of a genius."

Carlotta first soared for science, but the enchantment of the skies kept her floating. She kept a stable of over twenty balloons to choose from. Over a million people watched Carlotta fly across their cities during her thirty years of flying at fairgrounds and exhibitions. She found a freedom among the clouds that few earthbound women of her time were able to experience. Many women wanted to soar in Carlotta's boots—she made it look so easy. But it wasn't . . .

In an interview on the thrills and dangers of ballooning, Carlotta said, "There are times when one has to decide what to do and do it in the twinkling of an eye."

In the skies, Carlotta had to think and act swiftly to survive. She got swept up in a whipping cyclone, caught in a tornado, dragged across treetops, and lost above forest fires. Lakes were a problem because their currents were unpredictable. They could drag her craft downward, dunking her into cold, deep waters. This happened once with her seven-year-old daughter, Bessie. Her daughter gave up free-flying with Carlotta after that. But Bessie would still fly in captive balloons.

Carlotta loved making her audience happy and put them ahead of her own safety. Once at a flight in Ontario, Canada, a crowd of twenty-five thousand people had gathered. Some wild folks swarmed Carlotta's balloon and ripped it while Carlotta stood on a raised platform across the field. The massive crowd pushed in from all sides to see the skirmish. When Carlotta saw ladies getting crushed and fainting, she sprinted across the heads and shoulders of the crowd to reach her damaged balloon. She jumped in and launched—stopping the crush. Now her own life was at risk. The ripped balloon shot up to the skies and blew apart. Carl did not expect to see his wife alive again. But Carlotta thought fast! She climbed onto the concentrating ring, grabbed the balloon flaps, and used them as a parachute, landing safely in a tree. It was her first parachute flight.

And, during a new balloon test launch, the valve stuck. Carlotta popped up to the stratosphere like a champagne cork! Struggling to breathe, she raced to stop the expanding gas before her balloon exploded!

She later related to a reporter, "My eyes bulged out, the blood ran from my nose, my ears rang, and my cheeks flapped in and out like sails."

With her nerves of steel, she fixed the valve and wrestled her balloon down safely. Carlotta landed with a world altitude record for leaping four miles high in a natural gas balloon.

But one of the most unusual dangers struck terror into Carlotta when two electrically charged clouds grabbed her for a forty-five-minute game of badminton. The thunderclouds swatted her back and forth—eleven times!—before they let her go.

Carlotta recalled she was unharmed but "badly frightened by being made the plaything of such gigantic powers."

Other aeronauts might have died from so many dangers, but not Carlotta. Because of her laser focus, agility, and indomitable spirit, Carlotta always landed on her feet. Of course, she never stayed there for long.

CARLOTTA RETIRES (WELL, NOT QUITE . . . THERE'S THE BALLOON FARM!)

By forty-one, Carlotta was weary of the ups and downs of faraway fairgrounds and exhibitions. She was ready to drop anchor and retire. Sort of . . .

The Myers family bought a farm in Frankfort, New York. Instead of growing food, they grew balloons!

The Balloon Farm was a thirty-room Victorian mansion. Inside, it had offices, a chemical laboratory, and a printing press for advertising balloon ascents. There were carpentry and machine shops, shipping rooms, and a loft for laying out and cutting the balloon fabric. The house also featured rooms with gas-generating equipment. And yes, there were still rooms left for living quarters, entertaining, and reading. Carl and Carlotta took great pride in their aeronautical library, considered the largest in the US. In addition to books, journals, and magazines, it was loaded with albums of newspaper clippings of articles detailing the smashing successes and failures of aeronauts.

Carlotta and Carl's business swelled until most of the balloons sold in the US came from the Balloon Farm. They made, filled, and stored the balloons everywhere—down the ravine, in the barns, and, in the winter, on every floor of the house. Balloons were tagged with notes detailing their naughty or nice behavior after every flight.

Government officers marched to the Balloon Farm and ordered rainmaking balloons. (Carl had found a way to explode balloons to bring water down from the skies for thirsty lands.) They also came for war balloons which would help soldiers take the air advantage over enemies. Folks flocked to the farm in summer. Some came to work, some to watch, and some to test their own wild (sometimes feathered) flying contraptions. Even the soon-to-be-famous Wright brothers came.

Carl and Carlotta worked on their newest flying inventions, like the Skycycle. It was pedaled through the air like a bike. Their daughter Bessie flew it at indoor expositions. Brave ladies hopped aboard at Carlotta's flying school. Others dared only go 1,200 feet up with her on tethered flights. Carlotta kept her earthbound guests hanging on her every word with daredevil stories from her flights.

As time flew on, so did Carlotta. At sixty, she still floated freely in space, enjoying the view over her farm. In thirty years, she'd made over one thousand flights—more than any one man, and all the women of her time combined. She left no doubt that a woman could take charge on the ground and in the air.

Carlotta, Lady Aeronaut, nearly forgotten by history, earned her bows as a leading lady in the science and enchantment of the skies.

TIMELINE

Mary is used throughout this timeline but is interchangeable with *Carlotta*.

August 26, 1850—Mary Breed Hawley is born in Pennsylvania. [Author's note: Commonly mistaken as having been born in Boston or New York, census and other records show otherwise. Birthdate is based on census information and family records.]

November 8, 1871—Mary and Carl Myers marry in Hornellsville, New York.

1875—Mary and Carl move from Hornellsville to Mohawk, New York.

1878—Carl and Mary hire an acrobat and accomplished aeronaut, Professor Walliky Rulison, to ascend in their first balloon.

July 5, 1880—Mary's first flight at the Little Falls, New York, Fourth of July Festival. (Many accounts mistakenly state that she flew on the fourth, but she was referring to the weekend-long celebration of the holiday.) On this flight, she announces her performing name, Carlotta (used from this day forward). The lemon-yellow balloon was called the *Aerial*.

September 9, 1880—After taking off at a fair in Norwich, Connecticut, Mary is caught in a terrible storm. She barely survives after crashing into a basswood tree eighty feet up. She directs a group of baffled men on how to get her down.

February 1881—Mary and Carl have a daughter. They name her Elizabeth "Bessie" Aerial.

July 4, 1881—Mary opens the summer exhibition season with two flights on the same day in Utica and Hamilton, New York.

August 8, 1882—Mary's balloon is caught in a cyclone after launching from Congress Spring Park in Saratoga, New York. She has a harrowing flight but lands safely.

July 2, 1883—During an event in Ontario, Canada, crowds accidentally damage Mary's balloon. Twenty-five thousand people begin to crush the people nearest the balloon. To keep them safe, Mary runs from a platform, across their heads and shoulders, and jumps into the ripped balloon. The balloon soars two miles up. She forms it into a parachute and lands safely.

1883—Mary's book, *Aerial Adventures of Carlotta; or, Sky-Larking in Cloudland*, is published, giving a firsthand perspective on her flights and harrowing adventures. She is the only woman aeronaut author of her time.

May 26, 1885—Mary and Carl patent their Guiding Balloon Apparatus (US Patent No. 318,575). Mary is officially an inventor. She uses this revolutionary apparatus to surf the skies with precision. She can zigzag across the currents like a dragonfly and name the spot where she will land before taking off.

1886—Mary establishes a world record in Franklin, Pennsylvania, by reaching a height of four miles in a natural gas balloon. She also sets another record by traveling ninety miles in ninety minutes.

June 19, 1887—Over a million people have seen Mary's ascents, and more have watched her sail through the skies. She is called one of the bravest women in America.

July 18, 1888—Mary is challenged to a point-to-point race in her balloon the *Zephyr*. She flies above Brooklyn and lower Manhattan to Jersey City. Mary demonstrates to over three hundred thousand people that balloon travel is easy and efficient. She completes her route in ten minutes. It would have taken two hours for a traveler to complete the same route using a boat, a car, and a carriage on an elevated road.

September 26, 1888—Mary and seven-year-old Bessie launch together in a balloon race starting in Syracuse, New York. They crash into a nearby lake called the Devil's Punch Bowl. Bessie climbs onto a log and pulls them ashore.

October 1888–July 1889—The Myerses go on an aeronautic tour through France, Spain, Germany, and Russia. They also take orders to build balloons.

1889—Mary and Carl buy a home on five acres of land. They call their new residence the Balloon Farm. The Myerses launch a new aeronautical institution that manufactures balloons.

1891—Mary announces her retirement from exhibitions/festivals. She continues taking to the skies for pleasure, special events, balloon tests, weather research, and helping thousands of others ascend in tethered balloons.

1892—Mary is invited to submit a paper to the Chicago Aerial Navigation Conference of August 1893 along with other expert engineers and scientists. No other woman was known to receive an invitation to participate.

July 19, 1893—Mary and her dog, Columbia, are blown offshore while ballooning near Lake Erie. Mary drops her dog safely near the shore, but her balloon is whipped three miles away. She drops into the lake and is rescued by a tugboat after nearly drowning from exhaustion. Mary immediately announces her intention to continue her ascents.

June 12, 1912—Elizabeth "Bessie" Myers marries Newton Cordis Wing at the Balloon Farm.

July 13, 1913—Roger Hawley Wing is born. Mary and Carl become grandparents.

The Balloon Farm, Frankfort, N. Y.

Postcard of the Balloon Farm, Frankfort, New York. It was the only aeronautic institution of its kind in the world.

1919—The Balloon Farm becomes too much for Mary and Carl to manage. They sell it and move to Atlanta, Georgia, with Bessie and Newton, and Roger.

November 30, 1925—Carl dies at 83.

August 13, 1932—Mary dies at 81.

1998—The Balloon Farm is listed on the National Register of Historic Places in commemoration of the 150th anniversary of the first women's rights convention in Seneca Falls, New York.

SELECT BIBLIOGRAPHY AND SUGGESTED READING

All quotations used in this book can be found in the following sources marked with an asterisk (*).

*Bassett, Preston R. "Aerial Adventures of Carlotta, The Lady Aeronaut." *American Heritage*, August 1966.

———. "Carl E. Myers of the Balloon Farm." *New York History* 44, no. 4 (1963): 365–90.

———. "Carlotta, the Lady Aeronaut of the Mohawk Valley." *New York History* 44, no. 2 (1963): 145–72.

Buffalo Courier. "A Rattled Reporter: Carlotta Relates Her Strange Experiences in Cloudland." July 7, 1889.

Moolman, Valerie. *Women Aloft. The Epic of Flight*. Alexandria, VA: Time-Life Books, 1983.

*Myers, Carlotta. *Aerial Adventures of Carlotta; or, Sky-Larking in Cloudland, Being Hap-Hazard Accounts of the Perils and Pleasures of Aerial Navigation*. Edited by Carl E. Myers. Mohawk, NY: C. E. Myers, 1883.

Spellman, Jane, ed. *Women Belong in History Books: Herkimer and Oneida Counties New York 1700–1950*. Vol. 1, 2015.

Sun (New York). "Voyaging in the Sky." February 4, 1894.

Wright, Sharon. *Balloonomania Belles: Daredevil Divas Who First Took to the Sky*. Barnsley, England: Pen and Sword History, 2018.

A stereograph of Carl and Carlotta in front of the Aerial balloon (used for her first flight). These identical photos looked 3D when viewed through special glasses.

Broadbill featuring "Carlotta, The Aerial Princess"

SPECIAL THANKS TO

Carolyn Yoder and the Calkins Creek team; Anderson Abruzzo, Albuquerque International Balloon Museum (Marilee Schmit Nason, PhD); Crestlawn Memorial Park (Blake Blomquist); Dr. Mira Reisberg; the Hagley Digital Archives; Herkimer County Historical Society (Susan R. Perkins); Iacopo Bruno (WOW! WOW! WOW!); Jennifer Unter; the Library of Congress; Martin Schmitt and Jack Simons; Melissa Manlove; Peter Cuneo; Saratoga Springs History Museum (Jamie Parillo); the SCBWI (Lin Oliver, Stephen Mooser); Smithsonian National Air and Space Museum (Elizabeth C. Borga); Syracuse University Libraries (Julie S. Chambers, Kelly Dwyer); Troy Bradley/Rainbow Ryders (what a wonderful balloon ascent!); Vermont College of Fine Arts (Tom Birdseye, Jane Kurtz, Tia McCarthy): Manisha Patel; Maureen Charles; and the Wrights of the Roundtable. And to the extraordinary high-flying lives of Mary and Carl Myers.

To my *Skybound* girls: Jensen, India, Lisa, Emily, and Orly —*SGS*

To my inseparable copilot Francesca. And to whoever
loves to fly beyond borders. —*IB*

Calkins Creek
An imprint of Astra Books for Young Readers,
a division of Astra Publishing House
astrapublishinghouse.com
Printed in China

ISBN: 978-1-63592-815-0 (hc)
ISBN: 978-1-63592-816-7 (eBook)
Library of Congress Control Number: 2023905124

First edition
10 9 8 7 6 5 4 3 2 1

Design by Barbara Grzeslo
The text is set in Avenir LT Std.
The illustrations are done in colored inks on paper.